50 Years
OF CARING FOR SEAFARERS IN
PORT HOUSTON

David Wells and Jason Zuidema

50 YEARS OF CARING FOR SEAFARERS IN PORT HOUSTON

PUBLISHER
DR. JASON ZUIDEMA

EDITORS
Dr. Jason Zuidema and Dr. Michael Skaggs

AUTHORS
Rev. David Wells and Dr. Jason Zuidema

PHOTOGRAPHY
Louis Vest, Houston International Seafarers' Center, David Wells, Jack Thompson, Cite, Port Houston, Texas Catholic Herald, Seamen's Church Institute, NAMMA

DESIGN & GRAPHICS
Marie Cuffaro

In Partnership with

This publication is a special edition of The MARE Report, NAMMA's magazine to promote research for the benefit of seafarers' welfare professionals.
Opinions expressed herein are those of the authors and do not necessarily reflect the beliefs of *The MARE Report* or of NAMMA.
For guidelines or queries: executivedirector@namma.org

For other programs of NAMMA or more information on the organization, visit its website at www.namma.org.

NAMMA, 123 HAVEN, ST., P.O. Box 160, READING, MA 01867

President
REV. MARSH L. DREGE

NAMMA exists to provide a network for encouragement, training, and coordination of ministries that serve port communities in North America.

THE MARE REPORT © NAMMA 2019 ISSN: 2380-5765 ISBN-13: 978-0-9905823-6-6

Contents

- **4** Preface
- **6** Introduction: Seafarers' Welfare around the World
- **9** Early Days: Beginning Vision and Compassionate Care
- **11** The Church Responds: Ecumenism in Action
- **15** Laying a Foundation: A Powerhouse for Seafarers' Wellbeing
- **18** Getting with the Times: Adaptations to a Changing Industry
- **20** Many Parts, One Body: Contributions to Seafarers' Welfare
- **25** Charging into a New Century: Success and Evolution
- **29** A New Day: Seafarers' Wellness in a New Location
- **31** Personal Reflections
- **34** Port Houston Extras

Preface

With joy, the North American Maritime Ministry Association celebrates the 50th anniversary of organized care for seafarers in Port Houston. NAMMA's core objectives are to connect, provide opportunities for training, and encourage seafarers' welfare professionals in North America and with our partners around the world. We are happy to add this book to the growing body of print and web resources designed to stimulate conversations about best practice in service to seafarers. The history of maritime ministry at the Houston International Seafarers' Center has been so tightly woven into that of NAMMA in the past 50 years that a presentation of Houston history goes a long way to understanding the wider history of maritime ministry across North America.

As we complete this project on the history of ministry in Houston, we see clearly at least two strengths that have made Houston so successful: first, from its beginnings, seafarers' welfare in Houston has shown the value of partnerships, especially partnerships between the business world, the Port Authority, and the religious communities in Houston. Without these partnerships the project would have stalled or failed at several key junctures. The value of the Port Authority's willingness to partner with others throughout the history of seafarers' welfare in Houston cannot be overstated. Second, on a more profound level, the story of seafarers' service in Houston is about relationships. The story of the Houston International Seafarers' Center is not just about giving money or having lots of employees

Contents

4   Preface

6   Introduction: Seafarers' Welfare around the World

9   Early Days: Beginning Vision and Compassionate Care

11   The Church Responds: Ecumenism in Action

15   Laying a Foundation: A Powerhouse for Seafarers' Wellbeing

18   Getting with the Times: Adaptations to a Changing Industry

20   Many Parts, One Body: Contributions to Seafarers' Welfare

25   Charging into a New Century: Success and Evolution

29   A New Day: Seafarers' Wellness in a New Location

31   Personal Reflections

34   Port Houston Extras

Preface

With joy, the North American Maritime Ministry Association celebrates the 50th anniversary of organized care for seafarers in Port Houston. NAMMA's core objectives are to connect, provide opportunities for training, and encourage seafarers' welfare professionals in North America and with our partners around the world. We are happy to add this book to the growing body of print and web resources designed to stimulate conversations about best practice in service to seafarers. The history of maritime ministry at the Houston International Seafarers' Center has been so tightly woven into that of NAMMA in the past 50 years that a presentation of Houston history goes a long way to understanding the wider history of maritime ministry across North America.

As we complete this project on the history of ministry in Houston, we see clearly at least two strengths that have made Houston so successful: first, from its beginnings, seafarers' welfare in Houston has shown the value of partnerships, especially partnerships between the business world, the Port Authority, and the religious communities in Houston. Without these partnerships the project would have stalled or failed at several key junctures. The value of the Port Authority's willingness to partner with others throughout the history of seafarers' welfare in Houston cannot be overstated. Second, on a more profound level, the story of seafarers' service in Houston is about relationships. The story of the Houston International Seafarers' Center is not just about giving money or having lots of employees or an impressive building, but about connecting people. Because hundreds of staff and thousands of volunteers were willing to invest their time in this work for the last 50 years, more than two million seafarers have been welcomed in the Seafarers' Center and millions more have been cared for by chaplains and ship visitors throughout the Port : "I was a stranger and you welcomed me."

Thank you to the many people that have been involved in this project. It has been a pleasure to reflect on 50 years of history together. We hope that work for seafarers' wellbeing and ministry in Port Houston continues strong in the years ahead.

Thank you to Dr. Michael Skaggs, director of the Chaplaincy Innovation Lab at Brandeis University, and Kevin Walker, NAMMA executive assistant, for wonderful editorial assistance.

Dr. Jason Zuidema
NAMMA, Executive Director
Rev. David Wells
Chaplain, Houston International Seafarers' Center

Introduction

Being a seafarer is a difficult and dangerous job. Though standards and technology in the maritime world have improved markedly in the last generation, life onboard a modern ship continues to swing between periods of interminable monotony and intense pressure. With quicker ship turnaround times and increased paperwork, many crews find time in port to be where demands on their attention are most concentrated. The few hours they do have to get ashore are precious: there is no time to waste waiting for a lost taxi driver or searching in vain for a way to communicate with their families.

To respond to the welfare needs of seafarers, caring individuals around the world have set up port-based seafarers' welfare organizations. These organisations typically provide transportation, communication services, a drop-in center and, especially, a friendly welcome. Most of them are faith-based non-profits, many with histories stretching back into the early nineteenth century.

The earliest seafarers' welfare institutions were concerned with the challenges sailors faced when returning to port or in between voyages. Life as a mariner was especially difficult in the first half of the nineteenth century, made worse by criminals and gangs in port areas who were dedicated to taking money from sailors through deceptive schemes. Into the later nineteenth century and throughout the twentieth century, many of these welfare organizations were the first, and often only, line of defense for sailors in trouble. Many offered a clean, cheap, and safe place to stay in port and a staff that would make them feel at home. Many of the earliest institutions have persisted into the twentieth century, especially among Christian traditions.

Port-based seafarers' welfare agencies began to work much more closely with other partners from the wider community to provide practical help for seafarers. This practical support included the intellectual and social improvement of seafarers, eventually becoming less focused on religious or moral concerns and more on questions of housing and social welfare. With the notable interruption of two world wars, these models of religious and practical concern for seafarers that began in the nineteenth century continued until at least the middle of the twentieth century.

In the decades after World War II, the needs of seafarers changed dramatically. Many of the largest institutions were either too worn by war or ill-suited to changes in the modern maritime world. New ports and terminals were developed globally to accommodate changes in how ships loaded and unloaded cargo, especially after the innovation of shipping freight using standard-size containers by the American businessman Malcolm MacLean in the 1950s. Though various forms of containers had been tried on several ships before, the real launch of containerized cargo happened when McLean's ship, the SS *Ideal X*, sailed from Port Newark on April 26, 1956 to Houston with 58 containers. The idea of standard containers that could be loaded directly from ship to train or truck soon gained traction across the globe, with specialized container terminals becoming industry standard for the reception of goods of all kinds. These terminals were typically farther from urban centers and required enormous amounts of space to organize containers and allow gantries, trucks, and trains to unload. This move away from city centers, as well as the ability to load and discharge ships much more rapidly, meant that the traditional location of seafarers' welfare centers near old port areas also became less accessible.

In this period seafarers' welfare started to emphasize the so-called "seamen's club" as a central location for social services, moving away from larger hotel complexes from when seafarers had often spent weeks in port. Furthermore, as seafarers' unions became more organized and international maritime regulations stronger, the centers that made up welfare networks were tied into large global communities to more effectively protect and support seafarers. Short turnaround times in port coupled with greater stability and stronger labour protections in this period meant that seafarers' centers became a place to relax for a few hours and phone home, leading to such seamen's clubs springing up - including Port Houston. Long-established seafarers' centers often were remodeled to include a games room, a place to call home, and somewhere to enjoy snacks and refreshments.

EARLY DAYS: BEGINNING VISION AND COMPASSIONATE CARE

In the early 1960's, former seafarer and Houston businessman Albert Liedts told members of the World Trade Club (later called the Houston Propeller Club) that the Port of Houston was seen by seafarers as "the worst Port in the world." He had been a seafarer since age 16, and later a Chief Officer, so he knew what the seaman's life was like and how difficult it could be. After immigrating to America from Belgium in 1949, he settled in Houston in May of that year. He had visited Houston as a seaman in 1945 and believed the Port would soon boom. Liedts started his own business in 1958: The Port of Houston Transport Company. Already he was working to relieve some of the difficulty of the seafaring life and by 1956 he was taking magazines to crews on ships calling at the Port. He believed that Houston was a great port but lamented the absence of a seafarers' center to care for their personal needs, a safe place to go when not aboard. Liedts continued to reach out to seafarers in the Port of Houston. At Christmas time for a number of years, he and others would take cases of beer and magazines to the ships. These men would also assist seamen when they had medical needs. Their compassion moved them to do whatever they could to help, even using their own money to do it.

Liedts began the process to establish a seamen's center in Houston, but subsequent years would present many obstacles. In the meantime, Liedts and his group of business leaders held a meeting in November 1964, gathering several dozen people interested in the formation of a seafarers' center. A follow-up meeting occurred the next month, this time with local dignitaries and Coast Guard officers. The group recommended several possible locations to rent. A local architect was willing to donate his services for any remodeling needed if the center was established in an existing building. A representative of the Houston Parks and Recreation department had promised to make a soccer field available at Mason Park for all visiting seamen. The group discussed transportation options through public transportation, which might be set up for the city dock area.

In what would become the first in a series of bodies, attendees established an interim organization until a legal board could be established, with George Meerburg as President, F. Van Thompson as Vice-President, Sonny Flores as Secretary, and Albert Liedts as Treasurer. The new organization talked further about fundraising, but had no clear direction; nevertheless, on December 16, 1964, the group filed bylaws and other documents with the State of Texas to incorporate under the name "International Seamen's Center of Houston." Replacing the interim board was the first legally-established board of directors, including Liedts and a number of other maritime leaders. Later, this board asked Dr. Jack Brannan from Hermann Hospital to join them. Dr. Brannan was active in the Port and had been helping seafarers with their medical needs since 1939, and his experience and connections would add to the wide pool of talent that has typified the Houston board since its inception.

Knowing the enjoyment that seamen took from soccer, the new board arranged a match at Memorial Park in January 1965 between Dutch and Norwegian ships (the Norwegians won 5-2). Soon they approached Howard Tellepsen and asked for land that might be used for a seamen's center. In July, the Port and Tellepsen agreed to provide them with several acres at a nominal lease whenever the board was ready to build.

It would take hundreds of thousands of dollars to move forward with a building and more than just a board of directors to allow a center to function. Where would the rest of the money come from? Who would run the center? Despite the passion and enthusiasm of the board, the work stalled. By 1966, the group had fallen dormant. A driving spirit was needed to move the founding of a seamen's center forward. The answer to staffing and charity registration would be to partner with religious groups.

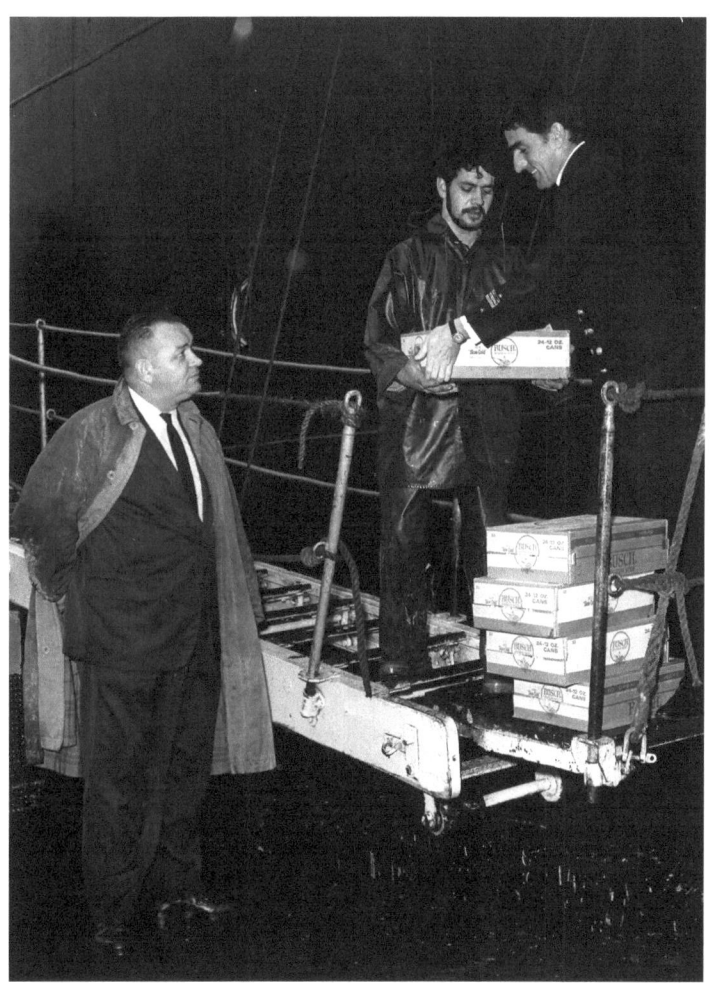

Left: Aerial View of the Turning Basin in the 1960s before Seafarers Center was built. (University of Houston Digital Library)

Above: Albert Liedts taking beer to ships, Christmas 1966 (HISC Archives)

THE CHURCH RESPONDS: ECUMENISM IN ACTION

While Liedts and the new board worked to establish a seamen's center on Houston's East Side, another group was addressing the basic needs of the marginalized in the same area. The Rev. Taft Lyon (Presbyterian), the Rev. Sam Duree (Methodist), and Fr. Rivers Patout (Roman Catholic) all had a passion for social service through the churches they served. They formally organized in 1967 by creating a multi-denominational group to build social service programs. The group was called T.E.E.M (The East End Ministry) and worked ecumenically to run camps, sewing classes, clothing closets, and other programs for those in need.

In late 1967 and after starting T.E.E.M., Lyon, Duree, and Patout all began to realize that there were ships docked along the ship channel and that seamen from all over the world worked on those ships. Only one of them - Lyon - knew what it meant to be a seaman and could understand how big a challenge this presented. When he was a student in 1948, well-paying jobs had been hard to come by. Lyon got hired for the summer to work as a messman by Socony Oil Company on a tanker making coastal runs for three months. The next summer, he sailed from a refinery in Beaumont as a wiper. Lyon later wrote that those jobs "prepared me for the later philosophic and concrete planning and development for the program and facilities of the Houston International Seamen's Center."

Lyon's interest in seafarers grew over time, but slowly, as he knew it would be a major undertaking. After serving as a pastor for several years, he had met a seaman at the World Mission Conference at Montreat, North Carolina in 1962. The seaman, Henk Weerkamp, was a member of the Dutch Reformed Church and was waiting to re-board a ship that would call again in a few months. Weerkamp had met several Presbyterians while touring the area; they brought Henk to the conference. Lyon asked Henk if his ship ever came to Houston; the Dutchman said that it did but that it had not done so for several years. Lyon gave Weerkamp his card and told him to call if he was ever back in Houston.

A short time later, in 1964, Lyon met two Dutch seafarers who were worshipping at his church, Trinity Presbyterian. One was Frank Cornelisse. The next day Lyon visited the men at their ship. Sometime later, Lyon was surprised to see Cornelisse interviewed on local TV for his opinion as a seafarer on why Houston needed a new seafarers' center.

In a short memoir written on how he became involved in the Center, Lyon recalled how these various "strings" were braided together by the insistence of seafarers: "In September or October of 1967, I received a phone call from Henk Weerkamp. The call went something like this: 'Hello, this is Henk!' 'Henk? Henk who?' 'Henk Weerkamp!' 'I don't know any Henk Weerkamp!' 'Oh, yes, we met at Montreat several years ago (actually in 1962), and you gave me your card and said to give you a call next time I was in Houston.' 'Oh yes, I remember now!' Henk, the engineer, was back in town and had kept my card in his pocket for five years waiting to give me a call! We had a fine visit!" Having this personal connection with Weerkamp and Cornelisse focused Lyon's attention on their needs. His interest was piqued in helping to build a ministry and a seafarers' center in Houston.

Rev. Lyon made some phone calls about the seamen's center issue as he had promised his friends Frank and Henk. To his surprise, he discovered that the Roman Catholic diocese had a small amount budgeted in 1968 for seamen's ministry and that the Lutherans, through the Norwegian Seaman's Mission, had a retired pastor,

Left: Japanese liner on Houston Ship Channel, 1963 (University of Houston Digital Library)

Above: Ad Hoc Committee on Seamens's Service Center (HISC Archives)

Taft Lyon presents to Al Liedts the first donation towards the new seafarers' center, a check for $5,000; June 1969 (HISC Archives)

Rev. Carl Zimmerman, funded to visit the Norwegian ships in port. By the March meeting of T.E.E.M. things were beginning to move. The pastors and their churches very quickly realized that there were few religious services to offer to seafarers, and this was an outreach ministry right in their midst. People from all over the world were passing through Houston with no one connecting with them or ministering to their needs.

The Church was ready to respond through these energetic men. They learned about Liedts and his group, who had already begun the foundation of a seafarers' center. At first, the business leaders did not want to join with the Church in their vision because they feared that it would prevent meeting all of the various needs of seamen, whom they felt wanted things beyond religion. No doubt the most serious question was about serving alcohol. But the Houston Seafarers' Center Board soon realized that in the Houston context, this hesitation was unfounded, as the three pastors were not as restrictive as Liedts and his colleagues had thought. The new center was to have beer and Bibles on offer.

In late 1967, T.E.E.M had begun talking in more concerted ways about seafarer needs in Houston, and Rev. Lyon, Fr. Patout, and Rev. Duree starting informing their individual church bodies about a possible common project. At the February 1968 meeting of the local presbytery, Lyon reported on the needs of seamen and for a seafarers' center. In his report he indicated that the Catholic bishop had already been made aware of the need and was allocating money for it. Lyon also reported that the Lutheran synod was working to respond likewise through the Norwegian Seamen's Mission. The presbytery recommended that the service committee contact nearby congregations and also to come up with its own plan for a seamen's center.

On February 19, 1968, an ad hoc meeting was held to discuss the need to minister to seamen with representatives from Presbyterian, Catholic, and Lutheran churches and also the Port of Houston. The group began planning how to proceed and scheduled a meeting with denominational leaders, community leaders, and the now-dormant board of the Houston International Seamen's Center. On March 4, an agreement was reached by which these businessmen and the religious community would work together. On March 15, an ecumenical Committee for Ministry was created with many of the same representatives of the February 19 meeting with representatives present from the Methodists, Southern Baptists, and the Disciples of Christ. The Seamen's Center Board and the ministry committee would now contribute to seafarers' welfare in two different, but complementary, ways. Each denomination participating in the ministry committee would provide and pay for its own chaplain, all technically independent but working according to a set of common guidelines. But they would also all lend support to the seafarers' center project and contribute manpower to make it run. They agreed that they were going to need a temporary location for an ecumenical seafarers' center, but that they also needed to cooperate to work on something more permanent right away.

In September 1968, to get started in a temporary location, the Seafarers' Center Board and the ministry group accepted the offer of the Roman Catholic Diocese of Galveston-Houston to house a temporary center in the upstairs space of the St. Vincent de Paul building on the corner of 67th and Harrisburg. The diocese also provided $2,000 to cover remodeling costs. By November, this temporary center was open for business. It was officially dedicated in an ecumenical ceremony on December 15, 1968.

Within a year, however, the facility proved too small. Duree reported in January 1970 that due to the increased demand from seafarers, "Our major problem, as of now, is space. The space we occupy now is entirely too small. We need to have two or three pool tables, and at least that many ping-pong tables. That is saying nothing about other activities that we would love to have, but have no room...we are desperately in need of finding larger quarters."

With the temporary location in operation, plans went ahead for a more appropriate and permanent seafarers' center. On October 3, 1968, the board had met to begin serious planning, with Lyon chosen as the key leader in development. Another meeting was held on February 7, 1969, with Howard Tellepsen present; the location of land previously offered was changed to Wharf 23, almost doubling the original offer of 4 acres to 7.92 acres.

On February 23, 1969, Lyon presented the full project to the Ministry Committee. He stated that the previous week the Port of Houston had leased to the Houston International Seamen's Center 7.92 acres of land for $1.00 per year for 50 years. That land alone was valued at $240,000. Yet the donation of the land was only a part of the overall project. The building itself would be $400,000, the outdoor sports facilities and landscaping an additional $330,000. In total the projected cost for the various partners was $970,000.

The Catholic, Presbyterian, and Methodist denominations were confident that they could find pledges of at least $150,000 for the building. In addition, in 1969, board member Dr. Brannan was contacted by Jane Dale (Blaffer) Owen, who was part of a Houston family known for philanthropy and the founding of what would become Exxon and Texaco - Dr. Brannan had been Mrs. Owen's mother's doctor for 25 years. Owen asked if Dr. Brannan knew how her family could make a contribution in memory of Norwegian Captain Torkhild Rieber, a family friend and the former head of Texaco who passed away in August 1968. Brannan told Owen about the effort to raise money to build a seafarers' center and introduced her to Howard Tellepsen, Chairman of the Commissioners for the Port of Houston. That relationship, and a December 1969 donation, encouraged Tellepsen on what became his part of the journey of building a seafarers' center. As Jane Dale Owen had promised to Howard Tellepsen a year earlier, she contributed $10,000 from her Family's foundation to the construction. Thus, the new center was shaping up to be truly a collaborative, communal effort, especially in material resources.

But the Houston Center Board hit another snag: due to changes in tax law, they were informed that the kind of organization they had set up in 1964 could not receive tax-deductible donations. In order to process tax receipts they would need to be refounded with religion as part of their charitable activity. On March 15, 1971, the center director noted in a report to the Ministry Committee an important change that solved the crisis: "One of the most important things that has happened is the solving of the problem at the International Seamen's Center of Houston. This corporation, which was to have constructed our new center, was declared to be non exempt by the Internal Revenue Service. This means that we could not receive funds from foundations. However, we have solved this problem by the creation of a new corporation known as the Houston International Seamen's Center. This is a bona fide religious corporation and has the blessings of the IRS." The center was back underway and the director was confident in the future: "At this time the swimming pool is under construction, and the batter boards for the new center are to be erected today." The soccer field had already been constructed and was being used.

Action at the Center in October 1972 (HISC Archives)

LAYING A FOUNDATION: A POWERHOUSE FOR SEAFARERS' WELLBEING

Aside from a building, one immediate need for the new ministry was a dedicated chaplain. Various parishes and denominations had pledged partial or part-time support, but it was insufficient to meet growing needs. The first full-time chaplain was the Rev. Tom Malone, a Lutheran. He began working in the spring of 1968 after returning from mission work in Nigeria. Carl Zimmerman, a Lutheran pastor who had the support of the Norwegian Seamen's Mission, joined Malone in visiting ships. By November, it was agreed that Malone and anyone working as a part-time chaplain or volunteer would meet weekly in order to coordinate their efforts. Volunteers from the different denominations also began to take an interest in the program, even when they had little prior knowledge of seafarers' needs.

In June 1969, the Rev. Sam Duree decided to make the seamen's ministry his full-time call. Eventually he was appointed as the Seamen's Center's first director and also served as senior chaplain. Duree and Malone described their work in a June 1970 article in the *Houston Post*: "Conversions to Christianity are 'very low,' Rev Duree said. 'Our major thrust is service.'" The article went on to mention that Duree and Malone agreed that the contemporary perception of seafarers was wrong: "Rev Duree, who is known more commonly as Sam, said he has never encountered any trouble from the seamen, on board ship or at the Center. Pastor Malone, agreeing there simply is no trouble with the seamen along the waterfront, emphasized that their image must be changed."

The growth of the ministry was spurred on especially by the growing number of ships from an increasing diversity of countries calling at the Port of Houston. The Ministry Committee noted these changes, observing in 1972 that "We are currently in a transition from a free-wheeling, frontier, extremely personal operation of 2 or 3 chaplains, to a more structured staff-operation of 5-7 chaplains, of whom 4 are full-time & paid and 1 is ⅔ time and paid. 1 of the 4 is on delegated duty with the Center as director. 2 chaplains are volunteer and part-time. We are currently without a Greek Orthodox Chaplain, a need we should fill on an urgent priority basis." With this new structure, the staff faced the problem of complete coverage of all the city dock area, plus the Lower Channel areas at a distance of up to 20 miles. That would take more energy and creativity. It seemed that new programs were being launched at each meeting; one meeting's minutes noted "In cooperation with the Norwegian Seamen's service who has loaned us a movie projector, a nightly movie has been reinstated and it is requested that the Committee reimburse the operator $2 a night for his services. The swimming pool heater is now in operation and the pool is open with a lifeguard. We are also feeling a pressure to have more and more flexible transportation facilities available." After having two full time Chaplains in 1969 activities began to increase. The Center moved sometime in 1970 to temporary prefabricated buildings at the Wharf 23 location. During that same time or shortly thereafter, the soccer field was built. Then after the soccer field was in use and before the main permanent building was constructed, the swimming pool was built. The building committee which had been created by Taft Lyon and Sam Duree in 1969 was well on its way to achieving many other details of what the new center would be like.

The ministry team grew enormously. In 1970, the Presbyterians added a full-time chaplain, the Rev. Tom Stewart. In 1971 the Rev. Roy Strange, who had served as a mission worker in West Africa for 17 years and spoke 7 different languages, also joined. Stewart captured the growing sense of connection with the Seafarers' Center in a comment from February 1972: "I find increasingly more of my time at the port is being spent visiting on board ships and telling the good news of the program of the Seamen's Center for the purpose of getting men to come to the Seamen's Center. I find seamen, both officers and men, to be well balanced, self-sustaining people, for the most part. What they need is a place where they can go that is decent, away from the 4 walls of a small room on board ship. This is the good tidings of great joy that I try to disseminate to ships of all nations and to the seamen of all nations."

The Episcopalians then provided a full-time chaplain, the Rev. Jim Scott, in January 1972. Later in 1972, the Roman Catholic Diocese of Galveston-Houston appointed Fr. Ivan Turic as a chaplain. Now there were six full-time chaplains from five different denominations. Chaplains and Center staff were also open to helping facilitate access to other religious services on request. Additionally, Scandinavian ships were being visited by the Norwegian church - at that time on Weir Street - by Rev. Sigurd Svendson and his assistant, Pier Andersen.

Port ministry was developing in the context of a rapidly growing city of Houston. Under Mayor Louie Welch, an effective, aggressive politician, Houston became a powerhouse of the American post-war economic boom. Houston doubled in size from 1940 to 1960. In 1963, Houston's population shot above one million, and by 1980, Houston would become the fourth largest city in America, where it still ranks today. The tenure of Welch from 1964-1973 saw the completion of the Astrodome, the Houston Intercontinental Airport, development of NASA's Mission Control Center, the reservoirs of Lake Conroe and Lake Livingston, and the development of the downtown core. Among all these projects was the cleanup and modernization of the Houston Ship Channel. The Sidney Sherman Bridge that carries an East Loop segment of Interstate 610 and straddled the Ship Channel started construction in 1969 and was completed in 1973. But in the decades after World War II the area of the port and the neighborhoods around it had not been welcoming to visiting seafarers. It was a neighborhood to be avoided if possible.

The Houston Ship Channel, finished in 1914, had already been open for more than 50 years by the time Louie Welch was mayor. Previous to the Channel's opening, goods could only be brought the 52 miles from Galveston to Houston by small barges on the shallow draft of the Buffalo Bayou. When it opened in 1914, the ship channel was hailed with a major celebration and parade; President Woodrow Wilson had a cannon fired via a kind of remote control from his office in Washington, D.C. to officially mark the ship channel open for operations. Over the years, the channel had been dredged and was functional for ships, but the area around the channel needed much improvement.

Work on making the

Left: Ships on Houston Ship Channel, 1962 (University of Houston Digital Library)

Above: Plaque from dedication of building at HISC (NAMMA)

channel more inviting fell to the Houston Port Commission Authority which, at the time, was under the chairmanship of Howard Tellepsen. Tellepsen was president of the family-owned Tellepsen Construction Company, appointed by his father Tom in 1940 and growing it considerably to be the major player in the physical expansion of Houston. The Tellepsen Construction Company had built many of the major hospitals, hotels, schools, churches, and other public buildings that dotted the Houston map.

As chairman of the ship channel commissioners and as part of the effort to clean up the image of the port area, Howard Tellepsen had communicated his interest in building a seafarers' center in the Port of Houston as early as 1965. He had a keen sense of public service as board member of several other charities, and knew about developing business as the president of the Harris Chamber of Commerce. As the Port developed many public and private docks during those years, he became uncomfortable as seafarers visiting the Port did not seem to be receiving any kind of warm, Houston welcome. He developed a passion for the project to serve seafarers, and his skills and capacity were uniquely capable of helping. But even more importantly, Tellepsen was a man of deep faith, active in the Episcopal Diocese of Texas.

Three or four of the denominations managed to pledge about $150,000 to the construction of the new Seafarers' Center and many smaller contributions were made, but these were but a fraction of the total remaining cost of the building project. The project would have stalled had not Howard Tellepsen taken a leap of faith - and for this he needed the advice of his father, Tom Tellepsen.

Tom Tellepsen was a counselor for Howard, but also a key encouragement for his maritime work. It was his father who had encouraged Howard to take up chairmanship of the Port Commissioners in 1956, even though this meant that the Tellepsen Construction Company would be prohibited from all bidding on Port infrastructure projects which ultimately spanned 14 years, Tellepsen had built the second dock of significance on the ship channel, Manchester Wharf, in 1922, followed by the Long Reach Docks for the cotton magnate Anderson Clayton in 1923. His father knew that investment of time in building the Port was worthwhile, because increased capacity in the Port went hand-in-hand with the growth of Houston. And Tom Tellepsen knew the maritime world well. Born in Norway in 1888, Tom sailed as a cabin boy at the age of 14 with aspirations of becoming a ship captain. Needing more funds, Tom sailed for America where the opportunities seemed abundant. After passing through Ellis Island, he honed his skills as a builder in New York and then on the Panama Canal project (the United States having taken over its construction in 1904), but found a permanent home in Houston in 1908, founding his own company, Tellepsen Construction Company, in 1909.

Tom Tellepsen's career started in shipping, but flourished in the construction of Houston. So, when his son Howard came to ask him for advice about building the new seafarers' center, the path was clear: "just go ahead and build it." Armed with the encouragement of his father, Howard Tellepsen took a leap of faith and pledged that his construction company would build the center even though only a part

Chairman Howard Tellepsen
(HISC Archives)

of the money had been raised. Construction on the main Seafarers' Center Building began in full force June 1972 and was finished by December 1972.

It was not just a simple building, but a center that offered activities and facilities considered to be state-of-the-art in seafarers' welfare. The new Seamens' Center included a full-size soccer field, outdoor lighting, a running track, a tennis court, a volleyball court, a large heated swimming pool, a locker room with a sauna, and more than 18,000 square feet of building space. The building was dedicated on January 22, 1973. The dream of a seamen's center had started in the business community, but it gained true force and sustenance from the Church. It was the energy of the Church (and the provided clergy!) that gave a soul to the Center.

The Center was officially opened in an outdoor ceremony on a surprisingly beautiful January day in 1973. Nearly a thousand people attended, including representatives from industry, labor, cultural communities, and many denominations. Delegates from Argentina, Belgium, Germany, Great Britain, China, France, Costa Rica, Italy, Guatemala, Sweden, Denmark, Finland, Norway, South Africa, Venezuela, Korea and Paraguay were present. The Austin senior high school band provided the music and a group of six "charming majorettes helped liven the occasion with their baton twirling."

A four-page special report was part of the next issue of the glossy Port of Houston Magazine to announce the opening of the "Friendly Home Away from Home." Mayor Welch declared the week of January 22nd to be "International Seamen's Center Week." He had sent his administrative assistant, Eddie Corral, to read a handsome letter for the occasion that urged "all Houstonians to visit their Port and this great new center and rejoice with us in offering seamen from overseas a true home away from home, full of the friendliness and hospitality for which our City and State are noted." Indeed, as the special report ended, the "Houston Seamen's Center is no longer 'on the way.' It is here! But it is up to interested Houstonians and, particularly, those allied to the maritime field, to see that this finest seamen's center in the world is kept alive and running."

Not reported in the Port magazine was that, besides that open-air celebration, the various denominational leaders had gathered to give thanks in a worship service as well. The worship service was also held on Monday, January 22, and featured church leaders who were integral for finding support and a number of chaplains who had begun to visit ships. The cross-section of chaplains was amazing for the time: a Methodist, an Episcopalian, several Lutherans and Presbyterians, a Greek Orthodox, and several Catholics. The standing committee of chaplains from this diverse group, working side-by-side, would have been almost unimaginable only a few years previous. It was not only the result of the confluence of cultures in a melting pot like Houston, the progress in ecumenical relationships throughout the twentieth century in the World Council of Churches, and the involvement of the Roman Catholic Church especially after Vatican II, but also an excitement that the shared words of the Christian faith might excite a common vision for service to other humans in need. The bulletin for the liturgy included the concluding note for

Seafarers' Center Dedication, January 1973 (Port Houston)

all gathered: "We sincerely hope that you will find time, and a way, to serve with us in this ministry to the men and women who sail the oceans of our Creator's World."

During that service Scripture was read, hymns sung, and the Gospel Lesson shared by the Most Rev. John L. Morkovsky, Bishop of the Roman Catholic Diocese of Galveston-Houston, who read Matthew 25:31-46. Afterward, the Rev. Taft Lyon, the Presbyterian chaplain, preached a sermon under the title, "The Earth is The Lord's."

Word of the Houston success in this ecumenical ministry spread fast. In the Houston Committee for Ministry minutes of the early 1970s, it was noted on several occasions that new centers were going to be founded soon in Port Arthur and Galveston, Texas, as well as ports beyond. After September 1969, Galveston leaders began to seek advice from Houston on a center in their port which might be ecumenical. In 1973, the Galveston Seafarers' Center opened, which still operates today. While Galveston is most heavily supported by the Catholic archdiocese, it continues to have an ecumenical board, receive donations from the broader church community, and hosts volunteers from many denominations.

As all these chaplains worked together and learned about other ministries in the same work, they discovered there were special skills and training necessary for this ministry. The Committee asked itself in March 1973: What kind of program do we want in the Center? How can our ship visiting become even more meaningful? Answers to these questions meant more focus on training new staff and volunteers. Such a training program did not exist anywhere in the world.

One Ministry Committee member, Roy Strange, was a man with a passion for education and learning. He began creating a training program for maritime chaplains in the Gulf Coast area and conducted the first three-day training program in October 1973. After discovering Strange's effort, the International Council of Seamen's Agencies (ICOSA - later renamed the North American Maritime Ministry Association - NAMMA) and the Apostleship of the Sea (AOS), which Fr. Patout had become involved in, asked the Houston Center to create a two-week training program for maritime ministry. The first Houston Chaplain's Training School was begun on September 9, 1974, with 4 students in attendance. The program has been offered nearly every year since and has trained over 300 people from around the world. Strange also wrote a manual for ship visiting, which was printed in several languages.

1974 and the years that followed saw the ministry's founders, Lyon, Duree, and Patout part ways. Lyon left the Houston area and moved to El Paso. Under his leadership, the foundational years had witnessed the creation of an organizational structure that made the Houston Center a model worldwide. Then in October, Sam Duree also moved on to other ministries. Duree had been the Center's director and senior chaplain for the first five years. He provided a steady hand in making and keeping the ministry ecumenical. The third founder of the ministry, Rivers Patout, had become a full-time chaplain for the center in June 1974. He would go on to serve for another four decades. He also served on the ICOSA committee for ship visiting and served on the steering committee of the International Christian Maritime Association, which had been founded in Europe in 1969. Patout became connected with many organizations and groups related to or interested in seamen's ministry—it was one of his many passions. In 1974, he was asked to speak with the Texas City-La Marque Ministry Alliance about the formation of the Houston International Seamen's Center and Ministry. After inviting him to speak to them, the Texas City-La Marque group decided to follow the Houston model and dedicate its own seamen's center in Texas City in October 1975. It was becoming clear that interest in seafarers' welfare work on the Gulf Coast of the United States would not be confined to Houston.

GETTING WITH THE TIMES: ADAPTATIONS TO A CHANGING INDUSTRY

ndividuals from the maritime industry and from the Church began to learn more and more about the lives and needs of seafarers. Seafarers were away from their homes and families for great stretches of time - often nine months or more out of the year. Boredom and loneliness have always been part of the seafaring life. A change of activity and environment, with new people to meet and interact with, brought out smiles and joy. Exercise and entertainment was a luxury rarely provided on board. Before the Houston Seafarers' Center opened, seafarers would walk off their ships and wander around East Houston with little knowledge of where to go or what to do. The paid and volunteer staff of the Center began providing guidance and transportation to address this lack. From its opening in 1972, nearby churches organized volunteers and youth groups to send to the Center. Teenagers and young men and women became friends to seafarers from all over the world. In 1973 alone, the churches sent over 2,400 volunteers to the new Center to serve nearly 43,000 seafarers. In a matter of only a few years of active ministry, Houston had developed the largest group of chaplains and volunteers of any seafarers' center and more ships being visited than any other port in the world.

During the Center's early years, ships' crews typically had a single nationality, with 40 to 50 men aboard. They often had several free days in port and wanted to leave the ship to relax or find a telephone to call home. The Seafarers' Center provided three public phones in 1981, with another three phones added later. The soccer field and swimming pool/sauna had been finished before the Center Building was even completed, and they proved extremely popular with seafarers. These amenities, which most would take for granted in any other community, put Houston on the world map for seafarers because they could now participate in organized team activities with other crews. The Norwegian Seamen's Mission, which shared part of the new Center's space, organized sport tournaments worldwide through the 1980's. In 1989, a covered pavilion and basketball court was built, and even received its own dedication ceremony.

Churches throughout the Houston area, from many denominations, began to ask for ways to contribute to this ministry. They began bringing Bibles, magazines, books, religious tracts and devotional materials, recorded music, taped movies, used clothing, and anything else which the chaplains might suggest could be given out. Chaplains distributed spiritual literature in over 40 different languages as seafarers requested it. Churches and community organizations began to sponsor parties and special events and dinners at the Center. Chaplains celebrated Mass for Roman Catholics or conducted worship services for Protestants, with the chaplain on duty providing whatever ritual he or she was trained to perform.

As time went on, work for most chaplains shifted from a focus on service to seafarers in the Center to service of seafarers on their ships. Ship visiting became a key activity for the whole chaplaincy team. A list of ships to visit was produced each day, with chaplains and ship visitors assigned to different parts of the Port at different times. After the ship arrived, the visitor would board at a convenient time (typically breaks or lunches) to welcome the crew and provide information on services. The visitor then would talk to the duty officer to confirm times when the Seamen's Center bus could pick up and bring them to the Seafarers' Center in the evening. The visitor would then stop in the crew mess room for conversation, especially with crew members who might welcome a chat with someone with local knowledge or the time to hear about their family joys and concerns back home.

Like the world of shipping, the work of seafarers' welfare in Houston never took a break – some of the busiest days were those on which others in the port or city were on holiday. The best was Christmas time. Not only did the Seafarers' Center offer regular services, but, like many centers around the world, the Houston team also organized a Christmas present program for visiting seafarers. As most seafarers come from countries with warmer climates, these gifts typically were warm hats, but also included toiletries, chocolate and a personal Christmas card. But it was especially the thought that counted: seafarers were uplifted that someone actually thought about them and would give them something to thank them.

Presents came from many local churches and other support groups. They gathered Christmas gifts in the form of shoeboxes or other small packages; chaplains could then take thousands of these packages aboard or offer them to seafarers visiting the Center. Support groups and churches have found this program rewarding even to the present. The Houston Seafarers' Center Christmas program became one of the largest in the world, today giving out more than 10,000 packages each year.

Chaplains sought to visit every ship as it arrived in port and to encourage seafarers to use the wonderful facility that now existed. One thing was distinctly absent from their work with seafarers: from the very beginning of this ministry, the work was not about converting foreigners to one particular church or religious observance, but rather service to seafarers of all countries and cultures. No doubt, each chaplain or volunteer represented the flavor of his or her church community, but on the whole the spiritual care of all seafarers required a broad understanding of people and faith. No individual chaplain worked completely independently, rather they all worked from a common understanding of the chaplain's role. Chaplains trained and retrained one another in weekly meetings, keeping current with new understandings about the maritime industry and problems for seafarers. The Houston chaplain committee was a truly ecumenical project, with no seafarer left out of the Center's care.

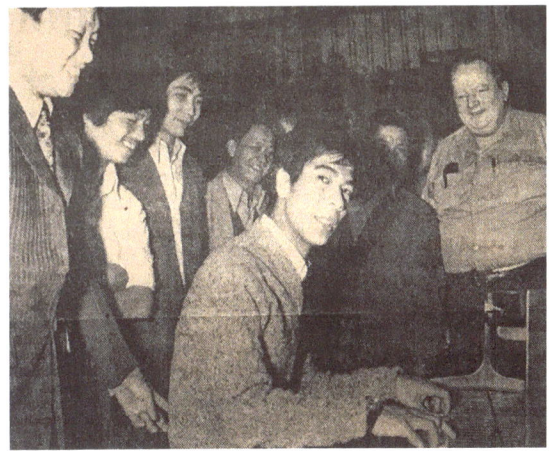

Left: Freight being loaded onto ship (University of Houston Digital Library)

Above: Chaplain Tom Stewart listening to Chinese rock, 1973 (Houston Chronicle)

MANY PARTS, ONE BODY: CONTRIBUTIONS TO SEAFARERS' WELFARE

Maintaining six or seven full-time chaplains from five or more denominations was a unique experiment in this very large port. The diversity of theologies and perspectives about ministry offered a rich opportunity for growth for each chaplain, and Fr. Rivers Patout provided a key influence to this success for over four decades. Fr. Patout was passionately ecumenical from the beginning of his ordained life; his personal style of compassion and openness in cooperative ministry helped to shape the Houston ministry. He was but the first of many Roman Catholics to be involved, with numerous other priests, deacons, and sisters ministering to seafarers from the Center's founding to the present. The first full-time woman chaplain, Sr. Rachel Smith, a Franciscan Sister from San Francisco, was appointed in 1979 after having served as an intern for a month in 1977. Some of the other full-time Chaplains were Fr. Luis Chia (1982-2003), Sr. Pamela van Giessen (1993-2006), Fr. Raul Marterior (2000-2002), Sr. Dominic Garcia (2001-2006), and Bro. Anthony Ornelas (2007-2014). Two Catholic seminarians have been sent to the Seafarers' Center every summer since 1970.

The United Methodist District provided other chaplains after Sam Duree left in 1974, with Rev. Bob Lowe (1975-1984), Rev. John Hassler (1985-1993), Rev. Mike McGraw (1993-2001) and Rev. Mike Scalora until 2013. At this point, the Bishop and Conference Committee decided that they did not have enough funding to support a designated chaplain - a substantial loss to the Center. However, individual congregations such as Faithbridge United Methodist and Cornerstone United Methodist continued to hold parties for seafarers at the Center and provide money for literature and video ministries.

Lutheran involvement began with the Rev. Tom Malone (1968-81) and the Rev. Andy Krey (1974-75), followed by a decade with no presence; a renewed commitment started again in 1991. Rev. Jesus Gonzales (1993-1995), Rev. Chuck Sheppard (1995-1999) and Rev. Ben Buehl (1999-2011) served as Chaplains. Rev. Sheppard, Rev. Richard and Marjorie Baker served on the Ministry Committee until 2017. The Lutheran Church is now greatly missed.

The Episcopal Church has been a part of the Seafarers' Center since the beginning, with Jim Scott serving as chaplain for thirty years beginning in 1972. He was appointed an Honorary Chaplain of the UK-based Mission to Seafarers in 1978. He was followed by the Rev. Lacy Largent until 2017. An Episcopal representative continues to sit on the Ministry Committee to the present.

The Presbyterians, especially the Presbytery of New Covenant, have strongly supported the Center from the ministry's founding, including the Rev. Taft Lyon and Rev. Tom Stewart (1970-1982) and Rev. Roy Strange (1971-1990). Other chaplains from the Presbytery have served, such as Rev. Rey Suarez (1990-1995), Rev. Dr. Ben Stewart (1996-2016), Rev. Steve Spidel (1997-1998) and those presently serving. Sustained Ministry Committee leadership has come from Rev. Art Allen (1973-2003) and Mr. Dwight Koops (2003-2017).

The Southern Baptist Church, the British Sailors' Society, a non-denominational Filipino church, and a non-denominational Chinese church are included in the churches, societies and denominations that have occasionally provided chaplains over the years. A rabbi served as part-time chaplain in the early years and a Buddhist couple has served seafarers in Houston since 2014.

The Houston Seafarers' Center has managed to retain at least six full-time chaplains over time. With this continuous leadership and the stable guidance of Fr. Rivers Patout, the chaplains conducted most of the ministry's work with less and less reliance on the Ministry Committee over time. By the late 1990's, the small group that attended the Ministry Committee monthly meeting dealt with little more than oversight of finances. Even this support soon no longer came from the churches but from programs conducted by the chaplains themselves.

But Fr. Rivers was the glue that held things together. Patout's service to the Lord focused on relationships with and between others. He looked for creative ways to serve others through Christ, exuding love, grace, and forgiveness. Over the decades he served seafarers, he worked two full-time jobs, serving a parish as well as the seafarers' ministry. He never seemed to choose one job over the other. Even while he served seafarers, he helped one of the parishes he pastored - St. Alphonsus - grow from a very small community to a parish bursting at the seams, with great increase in members and additional infrastructure.

In the early beginnings of the Houston Seafarers' Center, Fr. Patout was involved in organizations like ICOSA (later NAMMA), ICMA (the International Christian Maritime Association), and AOS (the Apostleship of the Sea). All chaplains working in the Houston ministry were strongly encouraged to be members of such organizations and Fr. Patout was known in all of them. This level of professional development raised the Houston Center's profile enormously, with the ministry unsurpassed in number of chaplains, contributions from industry and churches, and training for seafarer chaplaincy in the rest of the world.

The Archdiocese of Galveston-Houston's attention stayed focused on the Seafarers' Center through Fr. Patout's strong efforts. Every year a group of Catholic women came to the Center in December

> SPECIAL REPORT for DECEMBER
> Chaplain Jim Scott
>
> The joy of this ministry is a subject so broad that it would be impossible to cover all the aspects of it in a short report.
>
> The most important phase of our work as chaplains is ship visiting. There have been many accounts and analyses of ship visiting, but basically it is pastoral calling writ exotic. We share the same joys and sorrows and assist in the same crises (both trivial and profound) that the parish minister finds in his rounds. The only real difference is the crisis of time - because our parishioners are always moving on. We have to be ready to help here and now or to refer a seaman to someone halfway around the world. Follow up visits may be months apart - or the man may never come back - so we have an urgency for action that I, at least, never felt so pressingly in the parish ministry.
>
> One of the great advantages we have here that helps us deal with the crisis of time is our ministry team. I know that I can refer a seaman or pass on a situation to any member of our staff in full confidence. I can't be two places at once, but our ministry can be six or more places at one time dealing with different people or with different aspects of the problems of one man.
>
> It is this kind of team work that provides for me one of the great joys of this particular ministry. My special assignment as Scheduling Chaplain makes me especially aware of the depth of commitment of each member to the total ministry of the team. I often have to ask one chaplain to do a little extra so that another might be freed to do something special and I always find a willingness to co-operate and a concern for the total program that makes me very proud of our team.

Left: SS Rio Orinoco, 1955 (University of Houston Digital Library)
Above: Report of Chaplain Jim Scott, December 1972 (HISC Archives)

Christmas at HISC

to decorate, wrap Christmas boxes, and participate in a special Mass - a tradition that continues today. The Archdiocese has provided housing for many of the students who come to Houston for the two-week chaplain training course each year.

With one of the founders of the seafarers' ministry being a Presbyterian and with the Presbyterians having two full-time chaplains at the beginning of the 1970s, the Presbytery Service Committee always regarded this work highly. By 1976, a Presbyterian Seafarers Board was organized to oversee Presbyterian involvement. This board started with twelve members but has had more over the years. They met monthly to support the Presbyterian chaplains and to raise money from local churches. The board's support extended to other ministries, as well, including that of the Rev. Will Stambaugh (1988-2000) as chaplain at the Beaumont Seafarers' Center; they have worked in the past with churches in Port Arthur and Galveston to support those seafarers' centers as well.

While church funding for this chaplaincy began to slow down in the 2000s, in 2018 the Presbyterian Seafarers' Ministry received an endowment fund through the diligent service of board chairman Jim Keith to guarantee two chaplains in perpetuity. It will also allow for an intern every year in order to develop young seminarians who might find the work of ministry to seafarers as their calling.

Lighter moments punctuate this work, as well. In 2008, Keith suggested that during Christmas, churches from all denominations might use the M/V Sam Houston to sing carols to ships along the ship channel. With the support of the Port authority for the last 10 years, dozens of people from all denominations have sung to ships on two Saturday evenings in December.

During the early years, with chaplains organizing every working part of the Houston International Seafarers' Center as well as the Ministry, Sam Duree served as both senior chaplain and as Center director. Yet the bodies remained distinct, with an agreement by which "the secular group assumed responsibility for the physical plant and its operation, and the ministry group is in charge

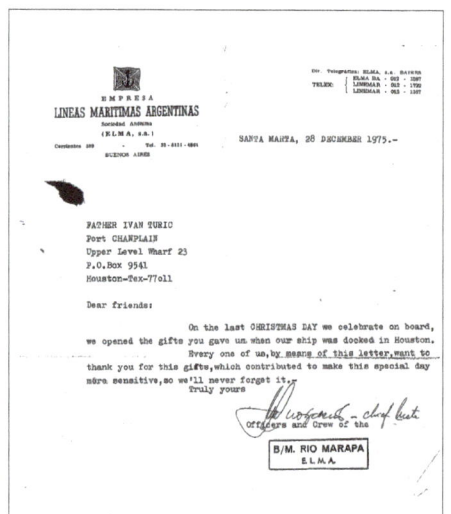

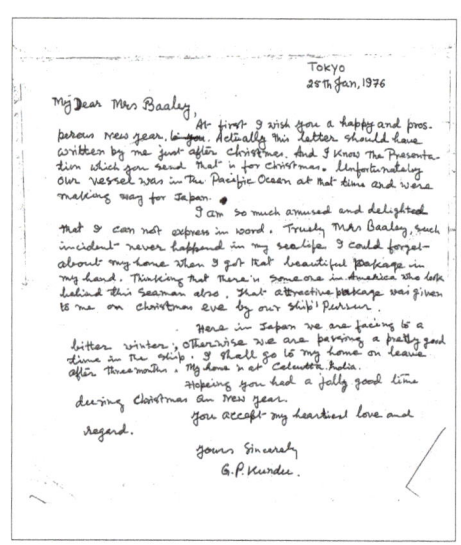

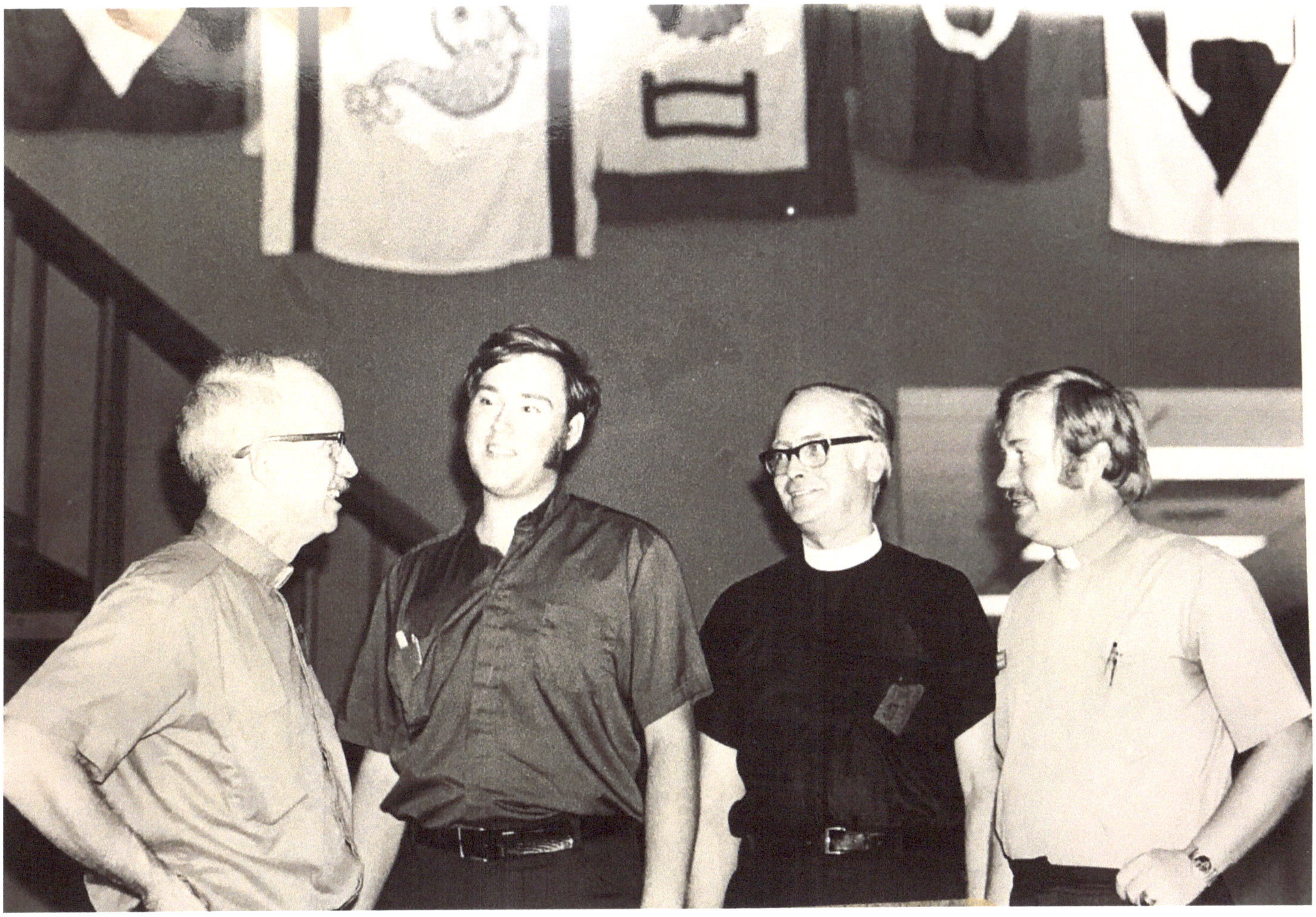

Roy Strange, Ron Bolinger, George Dawson and Rivers Patout, 1974 (HISC Archives)

of all programing. In other words, the secular group provides the building and the ministry takes care of what happens in it."

Chaplains were as tied to the various components of the maritime industry as they were to theology. The Church for these chaplains needed to understand the fundamentals of shipping, security, agencies, the Port authority, and seafarers. Even those within the local maritime industry began to see the chaplains as their "pastors" for events like weddings, funerals, blessings, and dedications, as well as for personal prayers and counseling. The maritime industry and members of the Houston Propeller Club (then called the World Trade Club) were a central and powerful foundation for the Houston International Seafarers' Center. Many companies and businesses showed great compassion for seafarers - this concern was not exclusive to chaplains. To this day, the Center's board includes volunteers from the maritime industry who continue to share the vision of the Seafarers' Center.

With chaplains tending to the wellbeing of visiting seafarers, the building itself needed to be taken care of and managed. Upon Duree's departure in 1974, Jack Hall rose from business manager to director. A number of directors have served since, with some overseeing expansions of the building and the board. The board itself has been active in connecting seafarers with the greater Houston area. One prominent example was the 1993 "Worldquest" program. After nine months of planning with the YMCA, Boy Scouts, U.S. Coast Guard, U.S. Customs, United Way, the Houston Port Authority, Howard Tellepsen, and the Center's chaplains, the board held camps and activities all summer for children throughout the area. Kids learned about seafarers, other cultures, and the work of the Port. Most importantly, all enjoyed a fun and supervised season.

OCEAN FLEETS LIMITED

Perseus

Algiers

30-12-75

Dear Padre

Please pass my sincerest thanks to the ladies of the Presbyterian church Houston for their wonderfull christmas present that they put on board this ship when we were in Houston back in early December.

If only they knew how much nearer home it made my wife and I feel — although we had presents from each other and from our families it was a really wonderful feeling to open a box from people that we hardly knew at all.

So we thank you all from the bottom of our hearts for everything — christmas and our happy stays in Houston. We hope that you all had a happy time and we wish you all that you would wish for yourselves for 1976 but above all Peace and Love. My wife and I are going on leave in January but we'll always remember the good times

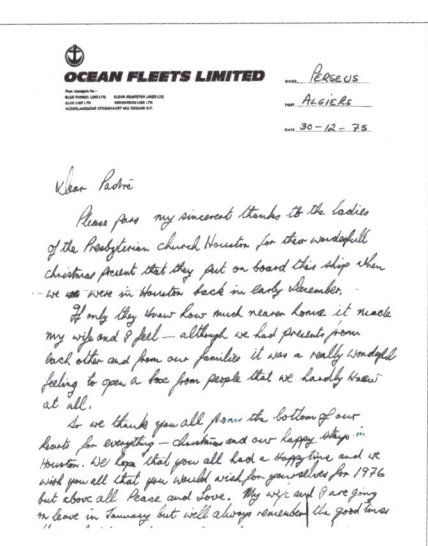

CHARGING INTO A NEW CENTURY: SUCCESS AND EVOLUTION

By the late 1970s, the Center's leadership realized that their success presented an opportunity to expand their public presence and fundraising in the following decade. In November 1978, an HISC newsletter noted "Since its [the Center's] dedication and opening five short years ago most of the cheap joints and dives in the waterfront area have disappeared. Houston was once called 'the worst port in the world for seamen' but now it is known all over the world among seafarers who look forward to their ship's next call in our Port." The Center received regularly letters of appreciation from shipowners and seafarers for the hospitality they received and the recreation they enjoyed.

Fundraising to pay off the initial construction of the Center was completed in 1981. On April 21, 1981, the Center held a special evening appreciation dinner to celebrate the final payment towards the approximately $700,000 cost of construction eight years earlier. But all those involved saw that more funding was necessary. Fr. Patout gave testimony May 26, 1981, before a committee at a national association of port directors about why a 'seafarer's welfare' fee should be included in a port's user's fee bill: "My testimony today will hope to substantiate the claim that a good seamen's center is one of the primary safety factors of shipping today, and in no way is such an issue as seafarer's welfare out of place in such a bill as we are discussing today. The human factor is the most elusive of all safety factors to control. To the chaplains and other personnel that serve in seamen's agencies, there is no doubt that the angry, frustrated, bored or mentally and/or physically ill individual is a threat to the safety of the ship. There is also no way one captain or agent with all the pressure to do 'business' while the ship is in port can attend satisfactorily to the personal needs of each crew member. And sometimes, although not frequently, the captain or the agent may be the problem. The Seamen's Center is the one best equipped to handle these problems, whether it is solved on a football field or in a counseling session." Patout's testimony might not have had the intended effect in other ports, but ships visiting Houston continued to pay the voluntary user fee with funding directed to the Center.

Other new fundraising initiatives were begun under the leadership of board and ministry committee members. The Center put on its first Maritime Festival and Shrimp Boil in 1984 and began an annual newsletter, which continued into the 1990s. Maritime companies from all over Houston became involved in Center events, putting up elaborate decorations, hosting competitive chili cook-offs, competitive industry team sports, and - most directly helpful to operations - brought thousands of dollars into the Seafarers' Center while having fun. Soon they also organized a fundraiser for the Center in the form of an annual golf tournament. Industry leaders were happy to contribute money for such events. Middle and lower level staff from shipping agencies and other companies volunteered and served on committees for the many activities. In 1987, the board and chaplains decided to hold the Center's first gala, which became one of the Center's biggest fundraisers.

Board, staff, and chaplains working together have succeeded through the years in making people and relationships the focus for the maritime industry and for seafarers in Houston. Business leaders in the Port of Houston have continued their contributions of financial support for the Seafarers' Center because of those strong relationships. The Port Authority has added further support by collecting the voluntary tariffs from ships that docked at the Port and transferring those funds yearly to the Center.

Others have been strong friends of the Center since its beginning. The Nolan Richardson family trucking business, located in 1972 across the street from the site of the new Center, long has supported this work. Patrick Cooney, a maritime attorney that Fr. Patout knew through the Notre Dame Club of Houston, has provided pro bono legal services for the Center over the years. Ms. Patricia Nemec has faithfully volunteered at the Center or its board since almost

Left: Houston Channel ship pilot (Capt. Louis Vest)
Above: La Porte Seafarers Center dedication (Port Houston)

Chapel at HISC (NAMMA)

the beginning. Furthermore, the strength of Fr. Patout's reputation has drawn connections to the Center from places quite far away. In 1984 a young Baptist chaplain serving seafarers on the Great Lakes, Marshal Bundren, called Fr. Patout for professional advice. The engaging priest invited Bundren to come to the chaplain training school in 1985; Bundren has been an assistant at the Seafarers' Center during school ever since. Men and women volunteering their time have gone on to become paid staff in several instances. Cathy Ulutas, for example, began as a volunteer and eventually ran the Center's store for almost 20 years. Gloria Falcon became volunteer coordinator and later managed the Center's books for more than 30 years of dedicated service.

The 1980s were a busy time for the Center. The Port of Houston was expanding, with more and more private and public docks opening farther east. Discussions even began about a second center in the Port of Houston. Roy Strange had become friends with a board member, Lou Lawler from La Porte. Strange convinced her that a center was needed in the her area. In 1981, an old house was donated and used as the first Barbour's Cut Seafarers' Center. That center was dedicated at a ceremony on November 18, 1981, with Jim Huller, director of HISC acting as master of ceremonies. Three years later in 1984, the Port Authority provided land on Barbour's Cut Boulevard, as well as a prefabricated 1,000 square foot building to replace the inadequate house. Volunteers in La Porte ran and supported the Center with Lou Lawler. Yet after several years that building also was not sufficient. The group later raised enough money to construct a new two-story building in 1993.

As one report put it, the crowd gathered for the dedication of the new building on June 4, 1993 was told that "after many years in a small, compact center that didn't have room to 'cuss a cat', the new structure was like walking into a palace." Marie Dennis, Center manager at the time, informed the guests that the new, large "Ships Store" area was furnished with fixtures and shelving donated by Walgreen's of La Porte. The wooden library furniture was donated by Jürgen Schröder, owner of Schroder Marine Services and president of the HISC Board of Directors. Many guests enjoyed the hand-made altar table and cross for the chapel, the cross being made from the porch rails from the previous, smaller seafarers' center.

In recognition of Ms. Lawler's significant service, the Barbour's Cut Center was renamed the Lou Lawler Seafarers' Center in 1996. When staffing at this location dipped below sustainable levels in the following years, the other Houston chaplains incorporated their own ship visits with the docks near the Lou Lawler Center. After 2006, the two centers became administered under the one executive director.

By the turn of the twenty-first century, seafarers' centers around the world had undergone great changes. Through the last decades of the twentieth century and into the twenty-first, many in seafarers' welfare saw a need to re-evaluate the approach focusing on recreation in seafarers' centers that had predominated since after World War II. As the turnaround time of ships in port decreased dramatically and mobile communications technology became more available on-ship, seafarers' drop-in centers with sports or recreation facilities were no longer as frequented as they once were.

Changes in shipping and seafaring were already in the air in 1980s and accelerated in the 1990s. Though one can point to many different factors driving change, a chief one was the result of ship owners favoring the registry of their ships in countries that had open registries, sometimes criticized as "flags of convenience." In the latter decades of the twentieth century, the trend was to register ships in this way, and so many ships were no longer crewed by single-origin communities. With ongoing developments in technology in the same period, crew sizes were diminished, as well, from 40 to 50 in the 1970s and 1980s to 25 or 30 by the next decade. Now, in the second decade of the twenty-first century, crews can be as small as ten individuals.

Some of this decrease was positive. With decreases in crew size, seafarers now had private rooms. Yet small luxuries like these were not without challenges themselves. After the September 11 attacks, security and restrictions within terminals made it more difficult for seafarers to leave their ships. Walking ashore became nearly impossible, and limited taxi transportation became very expensive. Furthermore, during the 2000s, as ships grew larger and more efficient, these reduced crews were required to work more hours, enjoy less free time, and feel more stress while in port. Efforts were made in some cases to improve life aboard: some ships had exercise equipment installed or a limited amount of Internet service to facilitate phone calls home. Internet and social media have evolved so that the outside world has been somewhat brought aboard. Yet these developments have been a double-edged sword: now with smartphones, private rooms, and less time ashore, the danger has increased for seafarers to become more isolated.

In the early 2000s, before every seafarer had his or her own phone, the chaplain team in Houston agreed to buy ten cell phones for seafarers to rent while in port. Soon enough seafarers all had their own phones, and developing technology led to more demand for Internet connections than phone lines. The Center reached an agreement with one telecommunications company by which the company agreed to give the Center unlimited data use for Internet hotspots for a reasonable price; the chaplains then replaced the ten phones with ten hotspots. Today, that number stands at twenty.

As time has passed, fewer and fewer seafarers come to the Seafarers' Center, with 40 or more per day during the early 2000s and now sometimes fewer than 20 per day. The broad variety of religious services which were offered in the Seafarers' Center itself before the turn of century narrowed considerably - a Catholic Mass on Sundays or a worship service when there was a special event at the Center with a larger group of seafarers. The Center's chapel is now most often used by seafarers as a private place for personal prayer. However, that has not meant services by chaplains are not offered. In the most recent period

HISC staff in Center store (HISC Archives)

24 passenger bus (HISC Archives)

of port-based seafarers' welfare, much more emphasis has been put on ship welfare visitor programs. These programs focus on transportation to local shopping, access to communications methods, and a friendly welcome to the Port. The Seafarers' Center itself is no longer the hub of activity; now, ship visitors and chaplains bring services directly to ships.

Fr. Rivers Patout died suddenly on June 2, 2014, leaving an enormous void in stability and leadership. While six full-time chaplains remained, the next years would show how much Fr. Patout had steadied the rudder of the ship and guided the team in remaining collaborative in this ecumenical ministry. Without the presence of Fr. Patout, certain challenges took more time to resolve than in previous years. If nothing else, it was clear that Fr. Patout had been an important gravitational force for recruiting and encouraging new chaplains.

A NEW DAY: SEAFARERS' WELLNESS IN A NEW LOCATION

The Center's board decided to move from the original location before the 50-year lease agreement expired in 2019. Times had changed and with fewer seafarers, the large and wonderful center of the 1970s was becoming less practical. The Port Authority agreed to continue a new lease for $1 per year at a new location a short distance down High Level Road, in a building shared with the Seamen's Church Institute's Center for Maritime Education. The Port Authority also agreed to pay for the remodeling of that space which opened in July 2017. Once again, the Seafarers' Center benefited from the hard work of a Tellepsen - this time Tom, Howard's son. The newly relocated Center brought its existing name with it, the Howard T. Tellepsen Seafarers' Center, in honor of that dedicated benefactor.

Tom Tellepsen had also entered the construction business; he also inherited the passion his father had for the Port of Houston. After his father's death in 2000, Tom became a member of the HISC board, with more hands-on involvement in the Center. He also worked regularly to raise money for the Episcopalian chaplain. Tellepsen was key in planning, contracting, and designing the new Center building, and made sure that details and history from the past building were connected to the new space when possible.

A final ceremony closed the era of the original seafarers' center. A decommissioning service for its chapel and the entire building took place on May 18, 2017. In January of the next year, the Rev. Rivers Patout III Chapel was dedicated in an ecumenical service at the new Center. The service emphasized the ecumenical and collegial nature of this ministry under Fr. Patout's leadership for 46 years.

Ministries like Houston's will always help seafarers to feel that their identity is affirmed, reinforced, and allowed to adapt through opportunities that can bring them acceptance, fun, and laughter. Sensitivity to other people and cultures is of great importance. Ship visitors and chaplains must always remember to listen for the seafarers' agenda before imposing their own priorities. In today's environment, time is even more valuable for seafarers than it was in the past. Seafarers' centers must be structured with opportunity, variety, novelty, and things which might be out of the norm for seafarers if they are to use their time to come to the center.

As load and unload times have become quicker and seafarers' free time has become more scarce, the focus of seafarers' ministry has shifted away from staying at the center and towards short ship visits. Seafarers' need for relationships with real people, counselling, and listening ears have remained the same. Chaplains and volunteers contribute most to the well-being of seafarers by striking up relationships with them during these short interactions. Simply being available to a seafarer and being interested in their lives go a long way towards making a seafarer feel valued. Chaplains and volunteers also minister to other people who work on the port, like surveyors, agents, terminal supervisors, Coast Guard inspectors, chandlers, transportation drivers, dock workers, security guards, port authority personnel, and many others. These are all small, yet very important, moments in people's lives. This work is so much more than just a narrowly defined job. It is an incredible calling.

Chaplains and ship visitors in Houston have a long tradition of reflecting their faith to seafarers but doing so with care. Being a faithful presence in the maritime community is something that each chaplain or ship visitor might interpret differently. Often, seafarers raise the opportunity to speak about their faith and the chaplain's faith; then, talking about these deep issues is powerfully important and meaningful for them. The work of a seafarer can often be challenging for the regular life of faith as they are far from their families and faith communities.

Even though it is not focused on the parish or congregational ministry that is central to traditional understandings of the Church, many have found the work of port ministry in Houston as one of the best outreach ministries available. It has reached people around the world in many cultures with less effort and funding than do the overseas missions of many of our denominations.

Chaplains to seafarers in Houston have served as very important connections to their own denominations. Local churches have been able to experience chaplains' passion for this ministry. Events for seafarers, specific prayer requests, and contributions have been pursued by chaplains in ways that respect congregations' abilities and outreach goals.

As the history of the Houston International Seafarers' Center shows, those who had been seafarers and who have worked with mariners felt a deep commitment to help them in a basic and human way. They joined together to work for seafarers with no benefit to themselves. Likewise, passionate and pastoral church leaders were deeply committed to working ecumenically as a group. They saw that being joined together in this ministry would succeed beyond any of their individual perspectives. They never let any one direction or a smaller focus on ministry dominate a rich and vibrant broader perspective. They worked closely with the business community to achieve deeper goals for the wellbeing of seafarers.

In the maritime world, one of the only constant factors is change. This means that our time, activity, and ministry may require creative and new ways to serve our Creator most effectively. Such creativity has driven decades of success in Houston and, with continued efforts, may see decades more.

Left: Ship on Houston Ship Channel (Seamen's Church Institute)
Above: Rev. Rivers Patout III Chapel (NAMMA)

Fr. Rivers Patout (Jack Thompson and Cite)

PERSONAL PERSPECTIVES

Rev. Mike Scalora
I received a phone call from our District Superintendent in May of 2003. He said, "We would like for you to go to the Seafarers' Center." I said, "Okay Jack, can I pray about it?" He said I could, but just a moment later asked, "Are you done?"

That June I reported to the chaplain's office at the Tellepsen Seafarers' Center. I was greeted by Father Rivers Patout and Sister Pamela van Giessen, who said, "You look pretty fit. You might survive."

The first few weeks were a whirlwind of activity. I shadowed experienced chaplains and worked Center shifts while completing the move to our new home, not far from the LaPorte Center on Barbour's Cut. For the next three years I enjoyed greeting and serving seafarers from all over the world, visiting ships and acting as host at the Center when mariners would come ashore.

The experience broadened and deepened my understanding of ecumenical ministry, as I had the opportunity to interact with people of all religious persuasions. The chaplaincy team - lay and ordained, Protestant and Catholic - worked together in a common ministry of hospitality, justice, and mercy. David Wells began a ministry of inviting groups from local churches to host parties for the seafarers, and I was glad to become a part of that work. In my third year at the Center I worked with Perkins School of Theology and served as the Mentor Pastor for ministry candidate and student Dan Gilliam. Dan told me later that his experience as a maritime chaplain was a wonderful preparation for parish ministry. I treasure that experience.

I left the Seafarers' Center when funding for a Methodist chaplain was discontinued and spent four years in medical chaplaincy. Returning to the Seafarers' Center as a ministry I had loved, I formed Bethel Port Ministries and remained at the Port of Houston for five years.

We served, we laughed, we squabbled, we shared joys, we shared disappointments. We weathered storms and mourned the loss of friends, but through it all God was with us. I now serve two rural Methodist churches, but always recall my days on the docks with joy.

Fr. Carlos De La Torre
I began this ministry when Father Rivers Patout passed away. He was well known to many throughout the ecumenical community. In addition to becoming a chaplain I inherited St. Alphonsus Church, becoming pastor to over 500 Catholics in the East End of Houston.

This ministry is very important to me because being Filipino myself, I can relate to the many visitors that come through the port. They are so far away from home, in a country they know very little about, missing their families, their food and their culture. It can be overwhelming to many, so we try to help them assimilate with their surroundings. I minister to all those different men by praying with them and hearing their stories or problems, or providing things like WiFi and SIM cards so they can have access to the internet and be close to their loved ones, which has a great impact on their relationships. I also try to use my vocation to guide them spiritually. Being fluent in English, Spanish and Tagalog helps me understand and speak with many more people. I enjoy visiting ships and this ministry has opened many opportunities to meet and share with others I probably would have never met. This ministry has also helped me grow in the understanding, dedication and commitment that is needed to be a chaplain to this unique community.

Fr. Jan Kubisa
I was born and ordained to the priesthood in Poland. In 1987, I went to Africa to do missionary work; I was then invited to work as a priest in the Archdiocese of Galveston-Houston. In 2004, I then joined the Apostleship of the Sea (AOS). Serving "all the nations" is a continuation of my missionary call. Seafarers from all over the world, as well as US merchant mariners, come to the Port of Houston year round.

When I first joined the team, I was told that our port ministry in Houston was the best organized port ministry in the world. The founder, Fr. Rivers Patout, considered the port ministry to be the most precious part of his work.

As a Catholic priest, I am in the front line of an essential pastoral service to seafarers. I often celebrate Mass on board. Occasionally, I help seafarers with the sacrament of reconciliation. I visit 5-10 vessels daily and bring the Good News in a simple way to thousands of hardworking people. Often, a little gift of the rosary or a prayer card, which I give while ship visiting, can make a difference in the lives of seafarers who are far away from home and at sea for weeks or months on end. In return, I receive a great gift of hospitality and gratitude from numerous seafarers.

There is a delicate balance between evangelizing and simply responding to seafarers' needs. There have been occasions when I celebrated Mass for only one or two seafarers, yet it was on one of those occasions that a seafarer said "it was the most meaningful Mass in my life." For me, that was truly rewarding.

Sometimes seafarers would like to come to our center, but they are stuck on board because they do not have access to shore leave. In recent years unnecessary restrictions and regulations have made it impossible at times for seafarers to go on shore. I am fortunate to be able to stay and pray with those people. It is truly a unique ministry of reconciliation for people who are marginalized by their situation.

In particular, I enjoy those moments when I speak Russian with so many East European seafarers. They open up whenever they hear their native language spoken. The seafaring communities from the former Soviet Union are God-fearing people. There are days in the Seafarers' Center when the majority of visiting sailors are from countries of the former Soviet Union and they truly enjoy using our facilities. The need for this ministry is so obvious and many seafarers reward us with their genuine gratitude for what we do.

Rev. David Wells
After my first year of seminary in 1975, I went to work for the summer in El Paso. There I met Rev. Taft Lyon, who had just left Houston to serve Manhattan Presbyterian Church after helping found the Houston International Seafarers' Ministry. As we sat in his office, he asked me what I wanted to do in the future and then asked me if I might be interested in seafarers' ministry. I had no idea what that was, so I said "no" and that seemed to be the end of it. Eventually I went to serve churches in Arkansas and Indiana; I later went to Thailand as a missionary. There, I lived in a poor village with 5 Christian families and 60 Buddhist families. I organized a Heifer Project to help teenagers raise cattle and worked with the pastor of a rural church in a nearby village. After 2 years, I moved to Chiang Mai to teach at McGilvary College of Theology.

In 1989, a serious accident impaired my ability to read and teach, and I returned to the U.S. I went to Houston in 1990, where a new Thai church was developing, and I felt that I could help that community. Upon arriving, I met Rev. Roy Strange, who had just retired as chaplain at the Seafarers' Center. He - like Taft Lyon had done years earlier - asked me if I was interested in seafarers' ministry. I still had no idea what this was and I told him "no" because I planned to help develop the Thai church.

By October 1998, I finished my work with the Thai church and had met Rev. Art Allen, who was then the Chairman of the Ministry Committee at the Houston International Seafarers' Center and sat on the Presbyterian Seafarers Board. In November, Art became the third person to ask if I was interested in seafarers' ministry. This time, I had no employment but still had no idea what this seafarers' ministry was. Art said, "Come volunteer for a month and then let me know what you think."

I had originally gone to Thailand to learn about God's presence in the midst of another culture. My wife and young family was a mixture of two cultures and two languages, and that was deeply a part of my life. Ideally, I was hoping to be a part of a ministry where I could affirm all of those things. In my month of volunteering I realized that seafarers' ministry was a relational and a counseling ministry requiring sensitivity to other cultures and other languages, as well as openness to other religions. It was a perfect match.

During my month volunteering at the Seafarers' Center, I got to know Fr. Rivers Patout. I found him to be a true colleague in Christ. I learned everything I could about him and the Center; I could never have found a better mentor. I also loved his passion for ecumenical and team ministry. Rather than trying to change people, he was more interested in loving them, caring for their needs, and serving the Lord in their presence—everything I would hope to develop in myself. I continue to strive today to emulate Fr. Patout's compassion and true concern for the wellbeing of seafarers.

Sr. Pamela van Giessen
I joined the Dominican Sisters of Houston in 1991 and was encouraged to become engaged in service. As I was looking for a full time opportunity for ministry I learned there was an opening for a chaplain at the Port of Houston. There I met Fr. Rivers Patout and was pretty much hired on the spot. This was a ministry that fit me to a tee: I spoke 6 languages, was familiar with foreign cultures, and it appealed to my sense of adventure.

During my time at the Center my duties encompassed visiting crews on board ships as well as staffing both Seafarers' Centers. We had six full-time chaplains and a few part-time chaplains; as a team we represented the major Christian denominations. We took turns carrying out other duties to ensure the smooth functioning of chaplaincy services. These duties included scheduling chaplain shifts, leading weekly meetings, organizing the annual retreat, and attending various seafarers' conferences and events, which were an important part of this ministry.

During the first years of my stay - before the advent of cellphones - the Center was always full of visiting seafarers. The place was hopping as seafarers came to relax, play pool, have a beer with crew mates, but also - most importantly - to call home. Night duty at the centers was a busy time. Sadly (for the Center), as technology improved we saw a drastic decrease of seafarers coming in to visit.

By far, my favorite duty was the ship visits. Especially in the early years of my ministry, there were many occasions on which chaplains brought not only spiritual relief but also helped to secure just treatment for seafarers. Many were the times when we encountered situations that reflected "the cry of the poor." We were the ones who would hear their stories. And we were the ones who could help, or who could find help for them. Sometimes seafarers didn't get paid, or their payment was late. Or seafarers were asked to stay on board longer than their contract stipulated. In those situations we tried to mediate or get help from organizations such as the Center for Seafarers' Rights.

There never was a dull moment visiting the ships and their crews from all over the world. The seafarers were almost always very welcoming; if they weren't, you knew there was a problem on board the ship! I enjoyed their hospitality; visits with captains, officers, and crews; and hearing their stories and sharing companionship and food. It was a great ministry!

There are so many stories I could tell, including the time I worked as a marriage counselor for a captain and his wife, who were in crisis; the time the captain of a ship told me the crew had planned to kill the first officer, who had been stealing their wages; the Turkish captain, a Muslim, who cried out "Jesus save us!" when he had a near collision with another ship; or the Norwegian officers who told me of pirate attacks and their preventive measures to keep them off the ship. Being a seafarer is a hard job: danger is everywhere, and injuries and deaths are not uncommon.

Rev. Tom Edwards
Following a career in business and service in the U.S. Navy, I spent 20 years in parish ministry. In the fall of 2013 some friends in Houston agreed to sponsor me to work one day per week with seafarers at the Port of Houston; most notable among this group was a former seafarer, Dwight Koops, who had chaired our ministry committee for 15 years. I interviewed with Father Patout, and then Lacy Largent, Ben Stewart and David Wells trained me. From the beginning I was hooked. As a pastor with a passion for cross-cultural missions, I have loved this ministry from day one. As Ben Stewart once said, "I get to be a missionary and go home and sleep in my own bed every night."

After a season or so, I was serving more days, substituting on a per diem basis. Then the Evangelical Lutheran Church of America (Gulf Coast Synod) sponsored me two days per week. Following that, a couple of grants were secured for more days and I was essentially full-time. In 2016, when Ben Stewart retired, I was appointed to his position.

This ministry gives me the opportunity to interact with some of the most incredible workers and interesting people from more than 70 countries around the world; to serve people not served; to minister to some of the hardest-working, lowest paid workers on earth, who provide 90% of the goods sold in the U.S.—to minister cross-culturally to "the lost and the least."

Further, I am amazed how reverent of God seafarers are and of their care and love for the world, as well as for their crew mates (their families away from home). To care for them and to help provide for their spiritual, social and practical needs is indeed a high privilege.

I try to bring joy and enthusiasm every day to this ministry. I keep a sense of humor about my calling, which is essential. My background in government, military and business adds a unique dimension. My theological training and global missions work gives me cultural sensitivity and valuable insight into the needs of seafarers. Most of all, I am teachable and learn more every day about how to better minister to seafarers. The ministry has not so much changed me as it reshapes me regularly — especially in my thinking and practice of this ministry. It is a very physical ministry and different every single day, which is the biggest difference from parish life.

Deacon Allan Frederiksen
Sometime in early 2006, Msgr. Ralph Salazar suggested there was a meeting I could attend and which would only require an hour each month; since I was a terminal manager at the Port, it would be convenient. I was then appointed as the Roman Catholic Representative for the Archdiocese of Galveston-Houston to the Ministry Committee of the Houston International Seafarers' Center.

After I retired from corporate life in July 2008, Father Rivers Patout, whom I had known for many years, suggested that since I was ordained clergy in the Archdiocese and a former seafarer, perhaps I should volunteer a bit at the Center. I did so, and Cardinal DiNardo made it a permanent social justice assignment. With the death of Brother Anthony Ornelas and, a few months later, of Father Rivers, I was appointed as a full-time chaplain at the Center. I served for two and a half years. At the end of May 2017 I left full-time ministry.

My time as a chaplain reinforced what I experienced during my many years at sea, working with people of many cultures, ethnicities, and religious backgrounds: we enrich each other by being able to listen, to hear what the other has to say. What did I take away from my experience? Perhaps what we encounter in all ministry: a feeling of being profoundly humbled. In most cases, seafarers bring God to the chaplain.

The Rev. Lacy Largent
(aka "Mother Lacy")
Episcopal Port Chaplain from
2/1/2002 – 8/31/2017
I was ordained in 1990, after seven years of service in the secular world as a clinical social worker. For the next eleven years I served as a hospital chaplain, a pastor, and a camp spiritual director. As a former social worker, I especially enjoyed my chaplaincy positions and the pastoral aspects of ministry. Ten years into my parish ministry, I was beginning to discern what God had in mind for me next. I began praying the Prayer of Jabez (1 Chron. 4:9-10), "Oh that you would bless me indeed and enlarge my territory," thinking that God might have in mind a larger parish in a larger city. Well, instead of calling me to serve a larger parish, God called me to serve the whole world as a port chaplain!

I was thrilled to become a port chaplain and absolutely loved serving the people in the maritime industry, particularly the seafarers. I saw myself as a world missionary without travel expenses! I woke each day eager to serve in whatever way God would put in my path: talking with seafarers and port workers, whether in distress or just in need of a listening ear; celebrating the Eucharist and other religious feasts onboard ships; helping host seafarers on shore leave; or representing the ministry to churches and maritime personnel. I loved learning about various cultures around the world as well as different religions. I became interested early on in tracking all that we did as port chaplains, so I began keeping statistics about how many ships were visited, whether the seafarers had visas and shore passes, how many seafarers were onboard, and what their nationalities were. Those statistics helped the Seafarers' Center document our work for grants from the Port of Houston and helped individual chaplains like me raise funds for our positions. I also served as the Bible chaplain, created PowerPoint shows for publicity, taught and helped administer the "Houston School," and filled many other roles - including the "Form Queen!" I loved getting to use my pastoral as well as my administrative gifts. I thank God for almost 16 years of getting to serve as a port chaplain!

Chaplain Thomas Tao
I became a Christian in 1965, after I realized and confessed that I was a sinner saved by God's grace. I first got involved with the seamen's ministry in 1988, when I saw a number of seamen had been brought to church one Sunday. They were brought by Lifeline to Seamen, an evangelical nondenominational nonprofit organization founded by Rev. Tom Malone three years before. I became very excited for this ministry, and began to visit ships and help bring seamen to church on Sundays.

In March 2003, I retired early from my architectural career to focus full-time on the port ministry. I received my M.A. in biblical studies in 2007, and my ordination as a port chaplain was in 2008. My life has been committed to bringing the Gospel to seafarers from then on. Rev. Tom Malone went to be with the Lord in 2010, and I picked up the baton to carry on the ministry. Mark Malone, Tom Malone's son, succeeded him as board director.

Lifeline to Seamen is supported by various local churches in Houston and partners with Christ's followers to take the good news of Jesus Christ to the seafarers that visit Houston. Our board consists of a director, five members, and now two full-time paid missionaries. From 2003-2018, we have visited more than 15,000 ships and witnessed to over 75,000 seafarers.

Rev. Dr. Ben H. Stewart III
In the fall of 1995, I was contacted by Bert Eakin and Bob Coller from the Seafarers' Ministry Committee of New Covenant Presbytery to interview for the chaplain position they supported. My interview included time at the Center and a ship visit with one of the chaplains at HISC, the Episcopalian Rev. Jim Scott. One month later I accepted the position, and I began my training as a chaplain the following spring of 1996. This meant a partial audit of the Chaplains' School and going to visit ships with the chaplains.

Ministry with seafarers has changed and expanded my worldview - even my approach to theology. Encountering the world in my backyard and being welcomed by Christian, Hindu, Buddhist, Muslim, and non-religious folks, on ships and shore, moved me to experience God in new ways. I can no longer live in a purely denominational, national, racial, or cultural silo. God in the world met me and said, "Come, eat, and drink in my world, which is full of many wonders and peoples."

I am not sure what my biggest contribution was to the Seafarers' Ministry. In the early days of the digital communication explosion I worked to get a computer - first just one for the chaplain, but then terminals for use by seafarers to send and receive email at the Center. This was our baby step into the brave new world of digital communication. Chaplain David Wells saw the possibilities beyond these steps and greatly expanded them with cellphone technology.

Retirement from this ministry was and is hard. The smell of the docks and ships, smiling at some known but mainly new faces is something I miss greatly. I have carried the expanded theological worldview into the current parish where I volunteer, and it serves me well. Larger than a neighborhood, a city, a state, or even a nation, I now see a world where God is at work, with me and sometimes in spite of me.

PORT HOUSTON EXTRAS

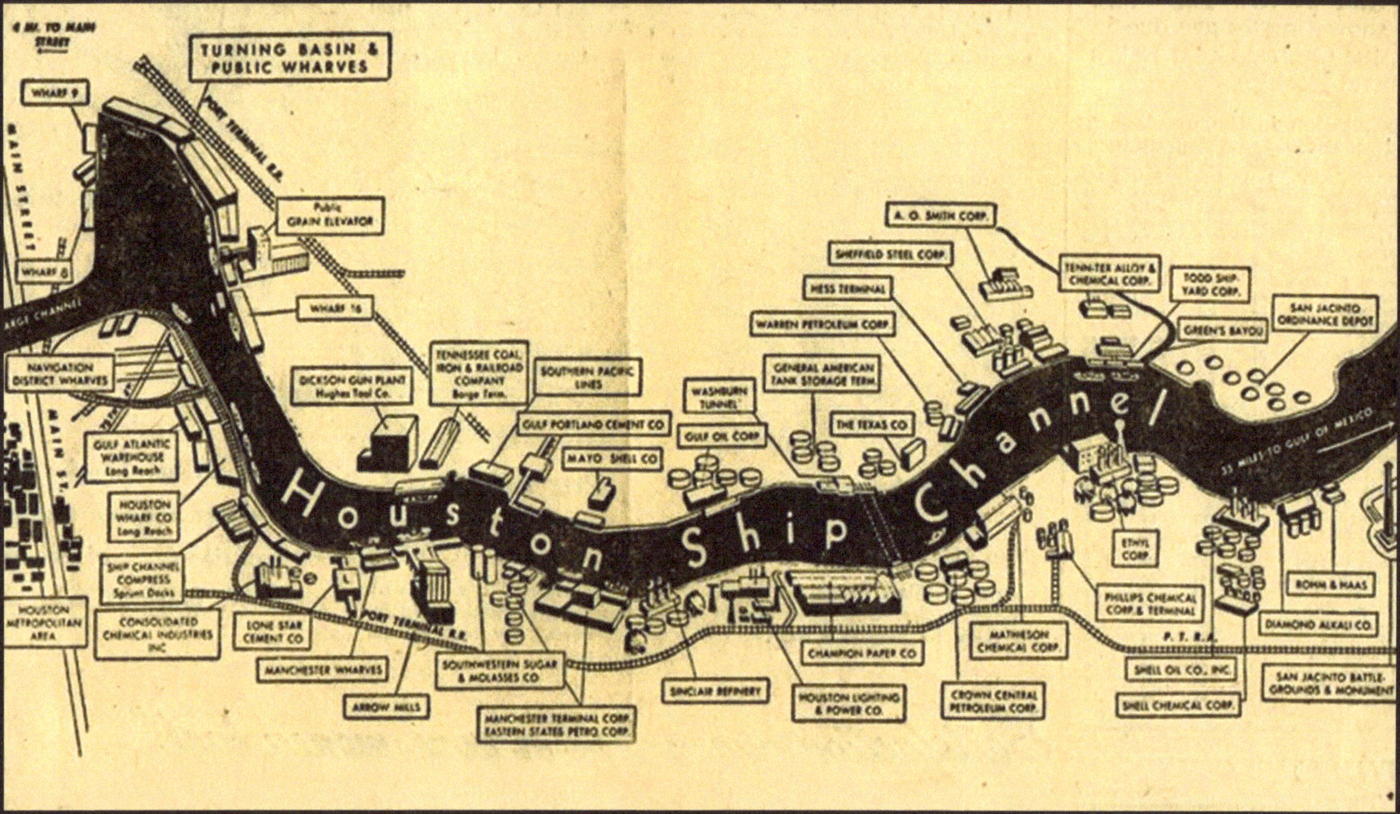

Houston Ship Channel, 1953 (University of Houston Digital Library)

Wharf 23 below the Houston International Seafarers' Center (HISC Archives)

Dig for Seamen's Center, 1970 (Houston Chronicle)

Rivers Patout and Patricia Nemec, October 1968 (HISC Archives)

Harry L. Webb, an American seafarer and member of Central Park Methodist Church, working at the Center in his time off from work in a ship's engine room, October 1972 (HISC Archives)

Sam Duree playing ping-pong with a seafarer, 1973 (Port Houston)

Relaxation at the Center in the 1972 (HISC Archives)

HISC Sports Week (HISC Archives)

Seafarers competing in Volleyball at the center in the 1980's (HISC Archives)

Seafarers playing Soccer in the 1980's (HISC Archives)

Seafarers' Center Pool (HISC Archives)

Front view of Houston International Seafarers' Center (HISC Archives)

Interior Houston International Seafarers' Center (Jack Thompson, Cite)

Jürgen Schröder honoring Lou Lawler, Gala 1992 (HISC Archives)

Tom Tellepsen II and Pat Cooney (HISC Archives)

Sam Duree, Rivers Patout, Taft Lyon (HISC Archives)

New Seafarers' Center sign (NAMMA)   New Seafarers' Center restaurant (NAMMA)

New Seafarers' Center interior (NAMMA)   Detail of Interior of Houston International Seafarers' Center (Jack Thompson and Cite)

The HISC community at the 2016 Houston School (NAMMA)

Houston Maritime Ministry training program, class of 1988 (HISC Archives)

Dana Blume, Jerri Parker, Tiffani Monzon, and Gary Krause (Wells)

Houston Maritime Ministry training program, class of 1992 (HISC Archives)

Left: Faithbridge United Methodist seafarers' party (NAMMA)

Above: HISC staff at 1996 gala (NAMMA)

Father Rivers Patout and Rev. Bob Lowe presenting Christmas presents in December 1976 (Houston Chronicle)

Chaplains Tom Stewart and Jim Scott, 1975 (NAMMA)

Memorial Drive Presbyterian Church delivering Christmas gifts (NAMMA)

Christmas gifts, 2016 (HISC Archives)

Christmas, 2015 (NAMMA)

Chaplain Staff in 2015 (NAMMA)

Christmas gifts for an Indonesian crew (Wells)

SPECIAL THANKS

Rev. Sam And Beverly Duree
Jim Keith
Dana Blume
Niels Aalund
Sharon Emerson
Dr. Paul Mooney
Tom Tellepsen II
Patricia Nemec
Gloria Falcon
Patrick Cooney
Jürgen Schröder
Marshal Bundren
Rev. Dr. Ben Stewart
Sr. Pamela van Giessen
Karen Parsons
Rev. Andy Krey
Rev. Lacy Largent
Thomas Tao

PHOTOS

Texas Catholic Herald
University of Houston Digital Library
Capt. Louis Vest
Seamen's Church Institute
North American Maritime Ministry Association
Jack Thompson - Cite
Port Houston

ARCHIVES

Houston International Seafarers' Center
Presbytery of New Covenant
International Christian Maritime Association
North American Maritime Ministry Association

UNDERWRITING SPONSORS

AET Inc. Limited
Apostleship of the Sea of the United States of America
Archdiocese of Galveston-Houston
Richard and Marjorie Baker
Buffalo Marine Service, Inc.
Ceres Gulf Inc.
David and Sharion Clark
Pam and Pat Cooney
Thomas and Lisa Damsgaard
Tom and Sherri Deen
Steve and Dana DuPlantis
Episcopal Diocese of Texas
Faithbridge Methodist Seaport
Welcoming Volunteers
GAC Agency Company Ltd
Greater Houston Port Bureau
Julia M. Haines
Guy Hitt

Houston International Seafarers Center
HISC Ministry Committee and Chaplains
Houston Mooring Co., Inc.
Houston Pilots
HUB International Insurance Services / Art and Sandra Flanagan
Inchcape Shipping Services
Genie and Richard Kobarg
Lawler Family
Lifeline to Seamen ILC, Inc.
Mangan Family
Maxcey Family
Memorial Drive Presbyterian Church
Patricia Nemec
Nordic Tankers
North American Maritime Ministry Association
Norwegian Seamans Church

Michael and Joyce Orlando
Carolene and Frank Patout
Jared Patout and J & Krystal Patout
Port Houston
Presbytery of New Covenant
Presbytery of New Covenant International Seafarer Ministry Board
Nolan and Bobbie Richardson
RightShip
Samunder Club of Houston
San Jacinto Community College District
Jürgen and Vera Schröder
Seaman's Church Institute
Steve and Brenda Stewart
David and Valanta Taveirne
Tellepsen Family
West Gulf Maritime Association
Marcus and Kim Woodring

www.ingramcontent.com/pod-product-compliance
Lightning Source LLC
Chambersburg PA
CBHW042029090426
42811CB00016B/1794